BASEBALL GENESIS

BASEBALL GENESIS

LIVING FOR CHRIST THROUGH THE GAME OF BASEBALL

TREVOR SANTOR

DEDICATION

I dedicate this book to baseball players from around the world whom desire to live a Godly-life, while pursuing their love of baseball.

Trevor Santor

Contents

INTRODUCTION

Baseball is America's pastime for two reasons: (1) the opportunity for underdogs to compete on a level playing field, and (2) the game's ability to effect social change in times of need. This great game has helped America break through the color barrier in the 1940's. It was also a catalyst when America needed a place to unite and sing the national anthem together as one nation under God after the attacks on 9/11. Baseball has always been a tremendous influence on this country then, now, and will be in the future. I believe the game's next big movement will be to grow God's kingdom through the game of baseball.

I know from personal experience that the baseball culture itself can be a very dangerous place to be if not careful. Many times a team can become a sinful congregation of young boys and men. Players and even entire teams can easily become entrapped in the slippery slopes of sin–a devastating place to be if the team is not aligned with solid Christian values and principles. I know this to be true because I was there myself through the fire, in high school and college, when I myself was a terrible sinner. Peer pressure and group-think were big influences on me during stages of life when new temptations were being introduced.

Just like in baseball, players need an offense, a defense, and a strategy to reign victoriously against the opponent. That is why the teaching and understanding of Christian principles is so crucial to the maturing baseball player today. Unfortunately, baseball players are growing up in a culture that is shying away from God. Baseball players' helmets of faith are weak, cracked, and even vulnerable to giveaway. But like all things, with Christ there is tremendous hope!

Since baseball has always been a platform where individuals have stepped up to lead others forward, I believe that baseball players can lead the charge and transform the culture with truth, not just for baseball, but for the whole world to see! From t-ball to the major leagues, God has equipped baseball players with the talents and abilities to perform and to be seen and heard by others. I believe God has given us these talents not only to play a great game, but to share with others the love of Jesus Christ. I believe baseball players from around the world can step up to the plate and lead their teams, their leagues, and their nations by setting the example of following the team captain of life who is our Lord and Savior Jesus Christ.

Not only can baseball give us an opportunity to demonstrate Christian character and apply faith through the game itself, but baseball can also help clarify our understanding of the Bible and its principles. Through baseball analogies, parables, and illustrations the game of baseball can help us practice and develop skills to live a Christ-centered life with our time here on earth.

Baseball Genesis is designed not only to improve our lives on the baseball field, but more importantly to grow

God's kingdom through the game. This approach to baseball and life will give us a solid game plan to defend against the tactics of Satan and the temptations of the world while growing God's Team of Righteousness. The analogies and metaphors in this book are exactly that, and are geared toward helping baseball players clearly understand the principles in the Bible. I pray this book will serve you as a strategy to grow in your faith and in your new identity in Jesus Christ, as it has in mine.

Blessings,

Trevor Santor

CHAPTER

THE BASEBALL PARABLE

The game of baseball is a sport that is highly dependent on one simple objective. If you can master this one objective and do it on a consistent basis you will have a much higher chance of succeeding in the game. This one simple objective is this–stay focused on the baseball. If you can stay focused on the baseball, you will hit the ball more consistently and make the plays that need to be made with fewer errors, thus helping your team win. Baseball and life are very synonymous in this one fundamental principle, and in this book you will discover why and how.

THE CREATION

Just like there would be no baseball game without the baseball itself, there also would be no life without God. For God is eternal, which means that God has always existed and will always exist. Yet, there was a point long ago, when

God decided to create the universe. So the question now becomes—why did God create the universe?

To help us answer this question, let us use a baseball metaphor. Imagine that there was only one baseball in the entire universe, and there was nothing else in existence besides that one baseball. No players, no bats, no gloves, no fields, nothing. Eventually, that one and only baseball with its almighty power decided that it would create a game that would revolve around itself. This game would be designed to produce joy, teamwork, self-discipline, faith, patience, and selflessness. Since there was no game, players, or field in existence, the baseball decided it would create those components. In essence, the baseball created a field, players, and a set of rules so that a game could be played and enjoyed by all who would participate.

This is essentially the same thing that God did with creating the earth, ˋhumans, and life. **"You are worthy, our Lord and God, to receive glory and honor and power, for you created all things, and by your will they were created and have their being."** (Revelation 4:11).

God created the earth and humans in His likeness so that He could (1) become a great coach, and (2) have a winning team that would produce champions of life. Not only did God create all things for His own pleasure and satisfaction of being coach, but He also made life for our own personal fulfillment and satisfaction as players in the game. The baseball would not have created the baseball game solely for its own pleasure, but also for the possible enjoyment of those who would participate, work hard, and play by the rules.

GOD AT THE CENTER

God did in fact design this life for Him to be at the center of focus, but let us not misunderstand the purpose behind why He did that. If the baseball created the game of baseball to revolve around itself, it did so for a very good reason. If the baseball players did not focus and keep their eyes attentive to the baseball while playing the game, then the players would end up making errors, striking out, and end up losing in the game.

It is the same principle with God and keeping Him in focus. God designed life for Himself to be at the center of attention not only for His glory, but for our own good to play this game of life correctly, avoiding the errors and injuries, and increasing our chances of winning. So for our own good, our joy, and our fulfillment, God desires us to keep Him at the center of focus in our lives.

OUR GOD IS THREE IN ONE

God, the Alpha, the Omega, the Beginning and the End, Yahweh. Our God has many unique names, but did you know that the creator of the universe is one God, but in three unique persons? There is God the Father, God the Holy Spirit, and God the Son. **"Then God said, 'Let US** make mankind in OUR image, in OUR likeness'..." (Genesis 1:26). This is called the Trinity of God.

Take a baseball for instance, it is one baseball, yet it is made up of three unique components: the core, the yarn, and the leather. Separately, they are individual parts, but when they are put together and laced up it becomes one whole baseball.

God the father is the core of the baseball; it is in the center and gives the baseball its solid foundation. God the Holy Spirit is the yarn of the baseball, which gives the ball its form and its innermost being within the ball. God the Son, Jesus Christ, is represented by the leather of the baseball, the flesh which was seen and felt in the physical realm. To complete the triune God, the red laces represent Jesus' blood that was poured out for us. **"...with his STRIPES we are healed."** (Isaiah 53:5 KJV).

Through this baseball metaphor, I hope you see clearly why Jesus Christ is God. Just like a baseball, **"Christ is the visible image of the invisible God."** (Colossians 1:15 NLT). Jesus completes the Trinity of God and His blood ties it all together like the seams of the baseball. Jesus had the Holy Spirit and the foundation of the Father within Him, and the Trinity was made complete by His blood. **"For in Christ all the fullness of the Deity lives in bodily form."** (Colossians 2:9). Each unique component put together makes the complete baseball, and each unique person together makes the complete God of our universe.

THE GENESIS

Long ago, God's original plan was to form a team in His likeness to coach, love, and reign as champions together. God desired His team to listen to Him, serve Him, and to remain in a loving relationship with Him. Like any good coach would, God desired His players to be successful and victorious in the game.

Also, like a very wise and experienced baseball coach, God knew exactly how the game needed to be played in order to win. Similar to baseball, when the players think they know more than their baseball coach they inevitably make mistakes and fail. Unfortunately, this has been the story of our human existence since the beginning of creation between God and man.

THE FIELD OF EDEN

In the Bible, the story of creation begins in the Garden of Eden. In Baseball Genesis, we will describe the Garden as the Field of Eden, a perfect pasture of land where God first created the game and recruited his first players onto His team. God created this wonderful baseball field with green grass, moist dirt, and level-ground. God separated the dirt from the grass, the foul territory from the fair territory, and put in the bases and home plate. **"And God saw that it was good."** (Genesis 1:18).

After creating the field, he recruited his first player onto the team and his name was Adam. God gave Adam permission to practice and play on the baseball field all that he wanted. With that permission God also gave Adam the responsibility to take care of the field by watering it, cutting the grass, and dragging the infield dirt. Then God told Adam that he is allowed to chew on anything on the baseball field, from bubble gum to sunflower seeds, but he must not chew from the leaves of the tobacco plant. For if he did than he would surely die.

Then God said, "It is not good for you to practice alone. I will recruit another player for you to practice with." Then God recruited his second player onto the team and his name was Steve.

THE FALL OF THE BASEBALL PLAYER

Now, the coach from the opposing team was very sly and he came by the baseball field and asked Steve, "Did God really tell you, you must not chew on anything on the field?"

Steve replied, "We may chew on anything on field, but God did say 'You must not chew on the leaves of the tobacco plant, and you must not touch it, or you will die.'"

"You will surely not die", said the coach. "For God knows when you chew on it, your eyes will be opened and you will become a better baseball player like God."

When Steve saw that the leaves were appealing to the eye and could increase his baseball performance, he took some and started to chew it. He then gave some to Adam who took it and started to chew. Then the eyes of both of them were opened, and they both began to feel sick to their stomachs. It was not before long that they started to vomit everywhere. Adam and Steve heard the sound of the LORD God as he was walking in the field in the cool of the day, as they hid in the dugout.

But the LORD God called out to Adam, "Where are you?"

"I heard you on the field and I was nauseous so I hid." Adam replied.

And God said, "Why are you nauseous? Have you chewed on the leaf that I told you not to chew from?"

Adam said, "The player you put here with me–he gave me some leaves from the plant and I chewed it."

Then God said to Steve, "What is this you have done?"

Then Steve said, "The coach from the other team deceived me, and I chewed it."

God said, "That coach will be sorry he ever stepped foot on this field. And for you two, go away and practice somewhere else, for I cannot have you on my field any longer."

They were kicked off the field, because they did not obey God's one and only command.

THE TESTING OF THEIR FAITH

Essentially, this is an illustration of what happened in the Garden of Eden in the Book of Genesis. Eve was deceived by Satan who tested the legitimacy of God's word by asking, **"'Did God really say...?'"** (Genesis 3:1). Eve was also deceived through her eyes of a pleasurable temptation. It says the fruit was **"...pleasing to the eye"** (Genesis 3:6). Eve was also deceived into thinking that she could be like God. **"'...you will be like God'"** (Genesis 3:5). This initial sin was the beginning of a pathway to death. When we sin, not only do we die a spiritual death, but it is also the path of actual physical death. This is true because one disobedient act leads to another, which leads to another. We quickly become slaves to sin and to death because sin is a vicious cycle that truly leads to death.

This sin cycle all started because Adam and Eve did not put their full faith and trust in God's Word. They did not fully trust in the legitimacy of what God said. This is the same problem that we face today, a lack of trust in God's word. If Adam and Eve had truly believed what God had told them, they would not have disobeyed and missed out on God's true blessings. But, since they disobeyed, God had to kick them out to teach us a very valuable lesson.

THE REBUILD

Ever since that point in time on the Field of Eden, God was planning a way to rebuild a team that would listen to Him, play for Him, and reign as champions in life. God used many men over the years to rebuild the team and to develop a godly team culture of obedience. Players like Noah, Abraham, Moses, David and God's only Son Jesus have been the players who have set the groundwork for God's team to rein as World Champions in life.

God's team began its rebuilding phase when God made a difficult decision to cut everyone from his team except one man named Noah. Noah was kept because he obeyed God's commands. After the cut, God made a promise to Noah that He would never cut His team off in that same fashion again.

God's team really began to grow strong when God recruited a player named Abraham onto the team. God told Abraham to take the team on a journey to find a field to call their home. So Abraham obeyed and led the team to conquer a small city on a hill called Jerusalem.

Jerusalem is where they built their home field and then decided on the team name. They would call themselves 'the Jews'. There were also other teams in the area that wanted to defeat the Jews, they were: the Egyptians, the Babylonians, the Philistines, the Persians, and the Assyrians. These teams had very outlandish team cultures and very wild strategies for playing this game of life. These teams were mighty in strength and in numbers. The Jews were not as strong in numbers or strength, but God wanted His team to develop an unshakable faith and trust in their teammates and in their coach.

God set up a 400-game series for the Jews to play verses the Egyptians at the Egyptians' home field. The Jews were beaten badly and lost the series. When they returned home to Jerusalem, God had a meeting with the team captain at that time, who was a man named Moses.

THE STRIKE ZONE OF LIFE

When God created life, He gave man freewill as part of the game's design. God gave man the ability to swing at any pitch that would come his way, but man must live with the results and consequences of his own actions.

There came a point and time when God's team became very selfish and undisciplined at the plate of life. Many players got themselves into the bad habit of swinging at terrible pitches that resulted in many outs. Many players were striking out in life, and many teammates would get upset with each other about which pitches were good to swing at and which pitches were bad to swing at.

During God's meeting with Moses on Mount Sinai, God gave Moses the boundaries of a strike zone. This strike zone was designed to increase their chances of succeeding in life by knowing the boundaries of a good pitch to swing at. This strike zone would make players more disciplined and overall better players in the game.

God called this strike zone "The 10 Commandments". Anything within the strike zone would be a good pitch to swing at and anything outside of the strike zone would not be a good pitch to swing at.

The Strike Zone of Life–The 10 Commandments:

1. Only one God; don't worship other gods
2. Don't make or worship graven images
3. Don't use God's name in vain
4. Keep the Sabbath day holy; a day of rest
5. Give honor to your father and your mother
6. You shall not kill
7. You shall not commit adultery
8. You shall not steal
9. You shall not bear false witness
10. Do not desire belongings of someone else

This strike zone of life was created to determine good pitches from bad pitches so that the team would have more success. It would take disciplined players to know the strike zone and to stay within its boundaries. Yet, if players remained patient and stayed within the strike zone they would inevitably become very successful in life.

This new strike zone created the need for umpires who knew the strike zone and would enforce it. In the Bible, these authorities of the law were known as Sadducees and Pharisees. These authorities studied the rule book and enforced them. They had the authority to call outs, decide on the outcomes of plays, call balls and strikes, and even eject players out of the game if they felt it was necessary to do so.

Like in baseball, some players had a hard time staying within the strike zone of life. Many players did not have the self-control or the patience to wait for a pitch within the strike zone. This created a negative effect on the team and many players found themselves in sin slumps that were very difficult to break out of. This is how sin works and how people become slaves to sin. It is like a slump that is very difficult to get yourself out of. The only way to break out of a sin slump is by following Jesus and keeping your eyes focused on God.

Jesus Christ, the only son of God, played His entire 33 year career and never found Himself in a sin slump. **"He committed no sin, and no deceit was found in his mouth."** (1 Peter 2:22). So take it from Jesus, learn from His teachings, and apply them to your life so that you will prosper. **"Follow the whole instruction the LORD your God has commanded you, so that you may live, prosper, and have a long life in the land you will possess."** (Deuteronomy 5:33 HCSB).

As a baseball player, it is in our best interest to know the strike zone and swing at pitches that are within the strike zone. In life, we are to take the same approach and know the strike zone of life and do our best to stay within those boundaries. It is God who made them, and it is God who knows what is best for us. It will take self-discipline, patience, self-control, and courage, but the rewards of staying within the strike zone will bring us great success and an abundance of joy. **"...in keeping them there is great reward."** (Psalm 19:11).

THE ONLY SON OF GOD

God had one and only Son whom He had trained to become the greatest player the world would ever see. God's Son possessed all of God's attributes and was born into this world as Jesus of Nazareth. Jesus grew up on the Jewish team and became one of the best players the team had ever seen. He performed miracles, always stayed within the strike zone, and never made a single error.

Soon, the Jewish team became a very hostile environment because the players only cared about their own personal stats and their own personal performance. Jesus was very upset with the leaders of the Jewish team because they simply were not being team players. The Jews cared more about their batting average, E.R.A., and fielding percentage than they cared about being a good teammate and helping the team win. The Jews were also very concerned about the possibility of getting cut from the team, so it was a very competitive environment.

This was not the original purpose that God had set forth for His team. Players were solely focused on the stat book, their own personal performance, and how God viewed them compared to others. It was not about being a good teammate or winning, which was the very point of God creating this game in the first place. The Jews made man-made rules for the team like not touching the sick or sinners, not eating certain foods, and excluding others from joining the team.

THE FORMATION OF CHRIST'S TEAM

God had plans to form a new culture that would transform the world. The plan would include His Son Jesus and the formation of a new team. The purpose of God sending His Son into this world was to form a new team of people who would choose to love God, love people, and focus on being a good teammate instead of personal performance. God wanted a team who would willingly give themselves up to move runners over, get them in safely, and pick up teammates when they would fail.

When Jesus turned thirty years old, He stepped out on His own and started to recruit players onto His very own team. Many players from the Jewish team would attend Jesus' practices where Jesus would preach. Jesus would say, **"Come to me, all you who are weary and burdened, and I will give you rest. Take my yoke upon you and learn from me, for I am gentle and humble in heart, and you will find rest for your souls. For my yoke is easy and my burden is light."** (Matthew 11:28-30).

Jesus recruited twelve players onto His team, also known as His twelve disciples, their names were: Peter,

John, James, Andrew, Philip, Bartholomew, Thomas, Matthew, James the son of Alphaeus, Thaddaeus, Simon, and Judas. These were the men that formed His new team and Jesus would teach them how to play the game of life the way His father intended.

The team leaders for the Jews at that time disliked Jesus because they thought He was a traitor and that He was putting the Jewish team at risk of falling apart. They were right because people began to follow and join Jesus' team.

The Jewish leaders could not believe Jesus was doing this, and they hated Jesus for it. So the leaders devised a plan to get rid of Jesus for good. The leaders convinced the other players that there was no possible way Jesus could perform so well in the game without the use of performance enhancing drugs. They agreed they would convict Jesus and accuse Him to the League of Romans of using performance enhancing drugs. If Jesus was found guilty of this charge it would mean termination from the league forever. This court hearing was held just one day before the Passover World Series of 33 A.D.

THE PASSOVER WORLD SERIES OF 33 A.D.

The biggest game in history, the Passover World Series of 33 A.D. was held in Jerusalem, it was a game versus The Jews and The Christians. When the League of Romans was notified about the accusations against Jesus, even from one of Jesus' teammates named Judah. The commissioner of the league, Pontius Pilate, demanded a drug test to be taken from Jesus. The results of the drug test would not be found out for another couple of days after the World Series.

Pontius Pilate held a press conference with fans of the league, and he let the crowd decide whether to let Jesus play or not in the World Series. It was decided by a roaring crowd that Jesus would play, but at a very costly price. Whenever Jesus would go up to the plate to bat, the pitcher from the opposing team would intentionally hit Jesus with fastballs without any penalty against them. Also, if the drug test came back positive and the Christians had won the game, then the title would be revoked.

THE ULTIMATE SACRIFICE

As the game went along, Jesus was brutally beaten with fastballs to His back, and was nailed from His hands to His feet. Then while Jesus was on base, they would intentionally hit Jesus with pickoff attempts to His side and to His head. Jesus was brutally beaten and could barely get up and compete for His team.

With the game tied in the bottom of the 9th inning with two outs and a runner on third base, Jesus walked up to the plate carrying His bat over His shoulder for His final plate appearance. Enduring the pain, and expecting another fastball to His head, He dug into the batter's box and prepared Himself for the pitch. When the pitch was delivered, the fastball came straight for His head, and in an instant, Jesus used the bat to lay down a suicide squeeze with two outs with the winning run on third. With every last bit of strength He had left in His body, Jesus sprinted down the line.

The pitcher fielded the ball, and threw it to first base. By a split-second, Jesus touched first base before the ball got there. "Safe!" The umpire called.

The run scored from third and Jesus had just won the World Series for His team. "It is finished." Jesus said.

Jesus collapsed due to impacts to the head and internal bleeding. Even though Jesus had won the game, the Christians were still concerned thinking the title would be revoked once the results of the drug test would come back.

To the surprise of many people, even the Christians, the drug test came back three days later clean and it was proved that Jesus was who He said He was: The Son of God, the greatest player to ever live, error-less, the MVP of life! Jesus and his teammates were crowned World Champions!

For FREE interactive videos inside of a private membership site visit: http://baseballgenesisbook.com/member

The Baseball Parable

CHAPTER

2

THE GEAR OF RIGHTEOUSNESS

The Christians became World Champions that day in 33 A.D. and still remain as champions today. The title can never be revoked, discredited, or abolished. The Christian team has grown and has become the light of the world and the salt of the earth. Players on the team are no longer carrying around the burden and guilt of sin or error, for we are no longer recognized by our statistics in the stat book of life, but we are now recognized as **"...more than conquerors through him who loved us."** (Romans 8:37).

Christians are identified as World Champions with Christ forevermore. This is because God had made a new promise, a covenant with the world and its people. The promise is that if you would accept Jesus as your Lord and Savior by faith, then you get to join His team, and God would no longer judge you based on your errors, but He would look to you as a World Champion in life!

A wonderful thing about the Christian team is that Jesus will gladly accept anybody whom chooses to believe in Him. He will never hold tryouts or make cuts from His team! The only requirement is that you believe in Jesus Christ! He is so good that He supplies His players with unending grace and mercy. All who are on the roster will remain on the roster forevermore, no matter the circumstances. **"All who are victorious will be clothed in white. I will NEVER ERASE their names from the Book of Life, but I will announce before my Father and his angels that THEY ARE MINE."** (Revelation 3:5 NLT).

RECRUITMENT

Since the World Series of 33 A.D., the Christians went out and recruited as many players onto the Christian team as they possibly could. The Jews did everything in their power to stop them, but God had other plans. Jesus went out and recruited a top player from the Jews to become a Christian. Formerly, his name was Saul of Tarsus, a top Jew who desired to defeat the Christians. Yet, on a trip to Damascus, on his way to defeat the Christians, Jesus stopped Saul in his path and proceeded to recruit him onto the Christian team.

Ever since that point in history, Saul was no longer Saul of Tarsus, but became the Apostle Paul, a devoted follower of Jesus Christ. Paul wrote many of the latter books in the New Testament and was one of the greatest players and leaders that Jesus had ever recruited. Paul's faith was unending as he persevered through many trials for the team to recruit many more players onto the Christian team. Paul was a top recruiter and a great addition to the team.

Jersey of Righteousness

Once we believe in our hearts and confess with our mouths that Jesus is our Lord and Savior, we are freely accepted onto God's team. A team that has conquered the world through one man named Jesus Christ. **"For it is by grace you have been saved, through faith—and this is not from yourselves, it is the gift of God—not by works, so that no one can boast."** (Ephesians 2:8-9). As a result of God's promise, the Christian team does not hold any tryouts or make any cuts. This is great news!

Everyone is accepted once we believe and trust in Jesus as our Lord and Savior through faith alone. He loves you just as you are, no matter how many errors or strike outs you have had in the past or will make in the future. He accepts you onto His team and will mold you into a better player each and every day through His unending grace, love and mercy.

When we first come to the cross of Jesus, we are wearing old uniforms that say 'ME' across the chest because that is who we played for prior to accepting Jesus as our Lord and

Savior. We played for our own fleshly desires. These old jerseys were never washed, they smelled gross, and they had stains and holes that were never sewn back together. On the day we accept Jesus as our Lord and Savior we get fitted for new uniforms. **"...put off your old self, which belongs to your former manner of life and is corrupt through deceitful desires, and to be renewed in the spirit of your minds, and to put on the new self, created after the likeness of God in true righteousness and holiness."** (Ephesians 4:22-23 ESV).

These new jerseys are made with an unbreakable fabric, and they have 'Righteousness' sewn on the front of them because that is how God sees us, as a righteous people! **"God made him who had no sin to be sin for us, so that in him we might become the righteousness of God."** (2 Corinthians 5:21). We are a people not represented anymore by our errors and mistakes, but are now known and recognized by God as believers in Jesus Christ, the one and only Son of God, whom God says he is *well pleased.* (Matthew 3:17). We actually trade our old identity and take on the new righteous identity of Jesus Christ! **"Because of his grace he declared us righteous and gave us confidence that we will inherit eternal life."** (Titus 3:7 NLT).

THE POWER OF A JERSEY

The power of a jersey has the ability to transform your identity as soon as you put it on. For example, let us imagine

26

that you are putting on a baseball uniform. First, you take off your old street clothes, and then you put on your baseball uniform which includes your jersey, your baseball pants, your baseball socks, and your baseball cleats. All of a sudden, something profound happens to you. There, in the midst of you putting on your uniform, a new identity and role has taken over you. You transform from just another person in the world, into a baseball player.

This happens all because of the jersey you have put on, what it represents, and the identity that comes with it. Here is the really astonishing thing–once you put on that baseball uniform, you start to feel like a baseball player, and then you start doing things that baseball players do. You begin to stretch, throw, hit, run, and catch the baseball like a baseball player would do.

This is the very same concept that happens to you when you put on the 'Jersey of Righteousness' through faith. As you take off your former ways and put on righteousness, you take on a new role and identity that is found in Jesus Christ. Soon, you start feeling and doing things that Jesus would do. You will literally begin to feel more righteous and act more righteously because of it! **"Therefore, as God's chosen people, holy and dearly loved, clothe yourselves with compassion, kindness, humility, gentleness and patience."** (Colossians 3:12).

This is the magnificent power of a jersey, and the jersey that Christ freely gives you at acceptance. This jersey that

Jesus gives you will have you feeling and acting more like Jesus simply because you are covered in His righteousness. That is the power of a jersey and that is what the 'Jersey of Righteousness' is designed to do in your life. It is designed to have you feel, and therefore live more righteously!

WASHING OF THE JERSEY

The wonderful thing about these 'Jerseys of Righteousness' is that every day we can ask Jesus to wash them free of all stains that come from the guilt and shame of our sins. If we confess our sins, it is like giving Jesus our dirty laundry, and He is faithful to wash them clean. **"If we confess our sins, he is faithful and just and will forgive us our sins and purify us from all unrighteousness."** (1 John 1:9).

As you know that after a few innings of playing baseball, our uniforms can get stained with grass, dirt, sweat, and blood. Living in the world is the same way. When we go out into the world, things can get messy quickly, and just because we are declared Christians does not mean our jerseys will never get dirty at the end of the day.

The great thing is that God says, **"Though your sins are like scarlet, I will make them as white as snow. Though they are red like crimson, I will make them as white as wool."** (Isaiah 1:18 NLT). Jesus wants us to know that our jerseys can be washed from sin each and every day. We get to wake up each morning to a clean and purified jersey! We no longer have to walk around with the stains of guilt and shame any longer, thanks be to God and His Son Jesus Christ!

YOUR GLOVE IS YOUR DEFENDER

In baseball, it is said that defense wins championships. This is as true in life, as it is in baseball. To be victorious in our Christian walks we need to consistently practice and work on our defensive skills to become great players in life. How we become great defensively in baseball is by practicing making plays using our glove. How we become great on defense in our spiritual walks is to practice using our Bibles to make plays. Using our bibles to make plays means knowing the Word of God and applying it to all circumstances.

It is difficult in baseball to make plays if we do not have our glove on our hand and having it opened. The same goes for wearing your glove in life. Wearing your glove in life means holding the Holy Bible in your hand and having it opened. **"All Scripture is God-breathed and is useful for teaching, rebuking, correcting and training in righteousness..."** (2 Timothy 3:16).

When we have our bible opened and we are reading it, essentially what we are doing is training for righteousness. We are getting work in so that we are prepared to make the plays when temptations are hit our way throughout our lives. When we are reading Scripture, it is equivalent to taking ground balls on a baseball field. This discipline needs to be part of our daily routine, because if we are not consistent in refining our defensive skills on a daily basis, by meditating on His word, we will inevitably make more errors. This is just as applicable in life, as it is in baseball.

The best defensive player to ever live was the Son of God, Jesus Christ. He did not make one single error for His entire 33 year career on Earth. Jesus was able to do this because He used scripture to defend against the attacks of Satan. When Jesus was tempted by Satan while in the desert for 40 days without food, Jesus would make the play every single time. Every time a temptation was hit to Jesus, Jesus would reply with "*It is written*", and then He would quote a verse out of scripture to make the play with. That is how Jesus made the play every time to defend against the devil's schemes. It is very similar to fielding a ground ball, and knowing what to do with it before it is hit to you, then quickly and confidently making the play.

Jesus is the only player in human history to ever live out a life without sin. Knowing this, we should take note on how Jesus played defense and follow in His footsteps. He knew what the Word of God said, and most importantly He applied it when a temptation came His way. That is how we must play defense in this game of life, having our Bible in our hands, having it opened, reading it, understanding it, knowing it, and most importantly applying it when the time comes and a temptation is hit our way.

When a temptation is hit your way, you must know what to do with it before it gets hit to you. You cannot simply run away from the ball and hide. It was hit to you, so you are responsible to make the play. You have to be bold and courageous enough to field it and get rid of it as quickly as possible. You cannot think about it too much when the temptation is hit your way because you do not have a lot of time, like a runner running down the line. You have to develop quick reactions, know verses, and apply them.

For example, if somebody is offering you to take drugs or drink alcohol and invites you to get wasted with them on the weekend, you should already know what verse to say in your mind, **"Be alert and of sober mind. Your enemy the devil prowls around like a roaring lion looking for someone to devour."** (1 Peter 5:8). Then simply decline the offer to that person in order to make the correct play. That is how we perform well on defense and reduce the errors we commit.

COMMITTING AN ERROR

Sometimes in life we do lose focus on God's Word and are not well-prepared to make the play. Here is what God says when we do commit an error, **"...forgetting what lies behind and straining forward to what lies ahead..."** (Philippians 3:13 ESV). God does not want us to dwell in the past, but wants us to focus on the next play that lies await in the future. God wants us to be players of adjustments from repentance. Repentance meaning we admit our shortcomings, recognize them, and most importantly learn from each of them. Every mistake we make can be used as teaching lesson to learn from and change our ways so that we will perform better in the future. Use the error you commit to your advantage by learning from it, then make the adjustments to do better next time, so that sin will not reign over you. **"Therefore do not let sin reign in your mortal body so that you obey its evil desires."** (Romans 6:12).

Remember that once you accept Jesus as your Lord and Savior, that God does not count our errors against us. **"...God was reconciling the world to himself in Christ, not counting people's sins against them."** (2 Corinthians 5:19). This will certainly help us to make fewer errors, not causing you to sin more. Like in baseball, when you are worried about your coach benching you or cutting you from the team for making an error, or striking out, the chances of you making an error or striking out increase because you have the worry and fear of the consequences weighing you down. On the contrary, when you know that your coach is full of grace, mercy, and love and will not punish you for the errors that you make, you are more likely to feel free, more confident, and perform better as a result. You will want to perform better for your coach. This is true because you do not have the overwhelming anxiety or high pressure of performing perfectly every time.

The same goes in our Christian walks with God. **"But now, by dying to what once bound us, we have been released from the law so that we serve in the new way of the Spirit, and not in the old way of the written code."** (Romans 7:6). God is no longer counting our sins against us, or is out to punish us for our mistakes. Therefore, it should take the overwhelming pressure off of us, thus creating a feeling of freedom that will produce actual results.

PICKING UP YOUR BAT DAILY

Every great hitter in baseball picks up their bat on a daily basis and swings it. The hitter takes his bat up to the plate when his name is called, and he uses it to hit the ball and help the team win. In Christianity, we must do the same if we wish to be great, but instead of a baseball bat, we are taking up our cross daily and following Jesus. Jesus once told a crowd of people, **"If any of you wants to be my follower, you must turn from your selfish ways, take up your cross daily, and follow me."** (Luke 9:23 NLT).

Taking up your cross daily means to acknowledge the sacrifice that Jesus willingly made for all of us on that day on Calvary Hill. Yet, it goes a lot deeper than that. **"Since we believe that Christ died for all, we also believe that we have all died to our old life."** (2 Corinthians 5:14 NLT). Taking up your cross daily means that we are identifying ourselves with Jesus' death, and His resurrection to new life. We are dying to our old ways of life, and its evil desires, and we are rising every day in new life in Christ. This is the identity exchange that we must commit to on a daily basis. When evil desires arise in our flesh, we must commit to the death of our old ways, and be born again in resurrection of new life in Jesus Christ.

"Whoever does not take up their cross and follow me is not worthy of me." (Matthew 10:38). If we do not take up our crosses daily, it is like a Major League hitter who does not participate in batting practice when his coach has asked him to do so. When the hitter's name is called for his at-bat, it would be like him going up to the plate without a bat to swing.

If a Major League baseball player, who gets paid millions of dollars a year did not practice his batting, or go up to the plate with a bat, which somebody else has paid for him to do so, then that player would not be worthy of the price that was paid for him. The same goes in our lives as Christians. It says in 1 Corinthians 6:20 (NLT) **"...for God bought you with a high price."** We must then honor and be worthy of that high price that was paid for us by picking up our cross on a daily basis and using it because it is our duty to do so.

Without the cross there would be no other way to get into contact with God. Like without a baseball bat it would be impossible to get into contact with a baseball that is pitched your way. **"Jesus answered, 'I am the way, and the truth, and the life. No one comes to the Father except**

through me." (John 14:6). Remember the importance of the cross and to pick it up on a daily basis, like Jesus did, so that we can remember who we play for and to live out our new identity as new creations on Christ's team.

HELMET OF SALVATION

In baseball, a helmet is designed to protect the baseball player from vicious blows to the head. It is durable to protect the baseball player's head and to keep the player safe from physical death. In the same way, the bible speaks about the 'Helmet of Salvation'.

The 'Helmet of Salvation' is very similar to the baseball helmet in the purpose that it is designed to protect a person from vicious blows to the head and keep them safe from spiritual death. Remember, our spiritual battles are being fought within our minds, and we are competing against an opposition that seeks to destroy us through evil thoughts and deceitful temptations.

So here is what it means to **"Put on salvation as your helmet..."** (Ephesians 6:17 NLT). It simply means to remind yourself that you have been saved once and for all through accepting Jesus Christ as your Lord and Savior. Once we accept Jesus as our Lord and Savior, there is no longer any doubt to our salvation and eternal life in heaven.

It is important to remember this truth when we are tempted to sin and the opposition is trying to convince us that we are not worthy of salvation and that we should just continue to live in sin. Remember, we are saved through grace, not by our works, or otherwise Jesus would have died in vain.

As a declared Christian, you have essentially declared war against the devil whose job it is to seek to destroy you. That is why we have to wear our 'Helmets of Salvation' daily. **"Put on the full armor of God, so that you can take your stand against the devil's schemes."** (Ephesians 6:11).

Satan will try and trick you into thinking that you are unrighteous and unworthy of the gift of salvation because of what you have done or continue to do in the flesh. But when we put on our 'Helmets of Salvation', we have tremendous confidence in Jesus because we know for certain that we have been saved, not because of what we have done or do, but because of what our Lord Jesus Christ has done for us. For it is written: **"...if you confess with your mouth Jesus as Lord, and believe in your heart that God raised Him from the dead, you will be saved; for with the heart a person believes, resulting in righteousness, and with the mouth he confesses, resulting in salvation. For the Scripture says, "WHOEVER BELIEVES IN HIM WILL NOT BE DISAPPOINTED."** (Romans 10:9-11 NASB).

For FREE interactive videos inside of a private membership site visit: http://baseballgenesisbook.com/member

CHAPTER

3

TEAM CULTURE

As believers in Christ, we have received the gift of salvation and eternity in heaven as members of Jesus Christ's team of grace and unconditional love and mercy. No longer do we need to worry about our statistics in life due to our performance of righteousness simply because that is not the focus of this team. **"Therefore, if anyone is in Christ, he is a new creation. The old has passed away; behold, the new has come."** (2 Corinthians 5:17 ESV).

We have become a new player who plays for a new team with a new mindset. So we have to learn the new ways of the team's culture and what the team represents. The team culture of Christianity is primarily focused on abounding grace, mercy, and love for all people of all races and nations. **"Your love for one another will prove to the world that you are my disciples."** (John 13:35 NLT). This renewal of our mind starts with first understanding who our God is as our head coach and authority in life.

GOD AS YOUR COACH

Let us first understand this one core concept which is that God is our head coach and authority in our lives. Nothing can be done without Him and He has power over all. In baseball terms, God writes the lineup cards, decides our positions, and determines who will be on our team. Let us understand then who our God truly is by first understanding His character.

In the book of Joel in the Bible, God is described in this way **"...for he is gracious and merciful, slow to anger, and abounding in steadfast love."** (Joel 2:13 ESV). This tells us that God is not like a head coach who easily gets upset and yells at his players when they mess up. The true character of our God is that He is full of abounding grace and love. When we do make a mistake, His desire is for us to correct it so that we can keep a happy, healthy relationship with Him and our teammates.

As members of Christ's team we have the opportunity to walk confidently up to God without fear of rejection and confess to Him our pains, our hurts, our worries, and our sins. He will supply us with what we need for spiritual, mental, and physical restoration and healing if we understand His promises and receive them. In order to receive His promises we must read His word.

God is a great head coach, but if we do not listen to Him through reading His word and studying it, how can we expect to gain any wisdom and understanding from Him? Let us be great players for God and listen to His word by diligently reading the instruction He has inspired for us. **"Keep this Book of the Law always on your lips; meditate on it day and night, so that you may be careful to do everything written in it. Then you will be prosperous and successful."** (Joshua 1:8).

Our God is a coach that richly supplies His players with what we need and righteously desire. The problem is many of us do not ask God to fulfill any holy wishes. God is very willing to supply His players with blessings, we just have to take responsibility to ask, and then receive them. Let us look at this from a different perspective. Would a good baseball coach deny his players from extra ground balls or a batting helmet that would protect them from serious injury? The answer is absolutely not; a good baseball coach would say yes and be more than happy and willing to go the extra mile and supply his players with all that they needed to be successful. How much more richly would a Holy God of the universe supply His own if only they would ask? **"Ask and it will be given to you; seek and you will find; knock and the door will be opened to you."** (Matthew 7:7).

FAITH AT WORK

God desires us to be blessed abundantly, but only when we ask and trust in Him completely. With all things concerning God, it takes faith for it to work. Jesus explains it best when He said, **"Truly I tell you, if you have faith as small as a mustard seed, you can say to this mountain, 'Move from here to there,' and it will move. Nothing will be impossible for you."** (Matthew 17:20).

Have faith means we have to believe in order to receive. Jesus also revealed to us that, **"...all things you ask in prayer, BELIEVING, you will receive."** (Matthew 21:22 NASB). Without belief or faith in God it is impossible to receive anything good from Him. So, in order to receive blessings, ask and always be confident in believing that God is at work in your life.

In the book of James, it talks about **"...faith by itself, if it is not accompanied by action, is dead."** (James 2:17). We cannot just expect God to do all of the hard work for us in our lives. God does play a big part, but we also play a significant part in achieving whatever it is we ask for. So do not be surprised when God expects you to put in some work for whatever it is you ask for. Just remember to always apply action accompanied with faith to see the results you desire from God.

God is a great head coach who is big on repentance, forgiveness, and mercy. At the same time, God also desires to mold you into the very best player possible, and that takes time and hard work. Imagine a baseball coach who did not make you run sprints, develop your stamina or discipline you when you disobeyed. It would be nice in the short-term, but in the long-run it would be a disadvantage to you because you would end up a below average baseball player. Remember that discipline is not a bad thing, for it is a good and necessary way to correct us and make us prosper in life. **"The people I love, I call to account – prod and correct and guide so that they'll live at their best..."** (Revelations 3:15-17,19 The Message).

God has sent the Holy Spirit into his player's hearts once we accept Jesus as our Lord and Savior and are baptized in the name of the Father, Son, and Holy Spirit. It says in John 14:26, **"But the Advocate, the Holy Spirit, whom the Father will send in my name, will teach you all things and will remind you of everything I have said to you."** God wants us to become elite players for Him, and that means accepting discipline, teaching, and rebuking for correction. God is a great coach, so let us trust Him that He is doing things for our own good.

If we recognize and accept God as our head coach in life, we will respect His authority and come to Him with our concerns, problems, and shortcomings and He is willing to help us. He is there for us at any time of day or night to give us what we need to be successful. It is like calling a timeout during a game to talk to our coach whether we are hitting, pitching, or on defense. So let us remember that we can call a timeout at any time in life and talk to God through prayer.

HONOR YOUR COACHES

Baseball Brethren, we must also remember to honor our very own baseball coaches who have been put in positions of authority over us. They have been given the authority from God, and we must honor that. **"All of you must obey those who rule over you. There are no authorities except the ones God has chosen."** (Romans 13:1 NIrV).

Let us not be like the lawless who show disrespect to their coaches by not following their instruction or speaking badly about them behind their backs. Let us be Christ-like in all that we do and show the utmost respect, dignity, and honor to those whom God has placed to rule over us to help us succeed.

As a player you should be watchful to serve your coach at every opportunity. You should constantly ask your coaches, "Coach, how can I serve you or the team today?" By practicing this servanthood, your coaches will gain a tremendous amount of respect for you. Also, your coaches will care for you deeply, and the other players will recognize that something is different about you. Players will wonder why you act in this certain way. This is a good thing because God has chosen you to be set apart and to show Christlikeness in your words, actions, and deeds.

THE DUGOUT IS YOUR CHURCH

As a Christian baseball player, your dugout becomes your church building. It is the physical structure where people congregate to meet, form relationships, and build a strong team bond before going out and facing the opponent.

It is very similar to the church building where people come together as a group to listen to the pastor, form Godly relationships, and a develop a team bond before going out into the world and facing the opponent. Therefore, treat your dugout as your church building and your teammates as members of your very own church. Some will be believers and some will be unbelievers, but treat them all with the love and kindness of Christ.

While you are in your dugout, seek to understand the members of your church and care about them as you would yourself. Seek to encourage them, inspire them, and always remember, **"...whatever you wish that others would do to you, do also to them..."** (Matthew 7:12 ESV).

LOVE YOUR TEAMMATES

The best way to become a valuable player on God's team is to love your teammates fully and unconditionally. We have been placed on our specific baseball teams for a much greater purpose than just playing the game of baseball. There will be plenty of lost souls on our respective baseball teams who desperately need to receive God's love, grace, and mercy more than we will ever know. More than anything, what they need is someone like you to come into their lives and show them the love of Christ through the kindness of your words and actions.

Eventually, when trust has formed in the relationship is when it would be best to present them an invitation to join God's team. Every one of us can help in God's recruiting process by developing a deep relationship with our teammates and earning their trust. Even if we do not get along well with them, or dislike their lifestyle or the way they treat people, we can still care about them as people whom God has created and desires to have join His team.

God recruits people onto His team through people who are already members of His team. You can become a great recruiter for God through being compassionate and showcasing His love. **"...to love your neighbor as yourself is more important than all burnt offerings and sacrifices."** (Mark 12:33). God is saying that His desire is for us to love people rather than attempt to please Him with any sort of sacrificial offerings. Let us not get too concerned about ourselves and our stat sheet, rather than seeking to help those whom have drifted far away from God.

Generally, the ones who treats us the worse will usually be the ones who need God's saving grace the most. **"Do not seek revenge or bear a grudge against anyone among your people, but love your neighbor as yourself. I am the LORD."** (Leviticus 19:18). God desperately wants to change the hearts of those on our baseball teams through knowing Him and choosing to follow Him.

Whether we know it or not, our teammates struggle with pains, hurts, losses, addictions, and sin that only God has the power to restore. Many times our teammates will take their hurts out on those who are closest to them in proximity; this could very likely mean you. I urge you, brothers, do not take any attacks personally, but give the burdens to God because most people are lost and God desperately wants to change them from the inside out.

LOVE YOUR ENEMY

We know that it is God's desire to recruit all people onto His team and change their hearts and their identity forevermore. It says in 1 Timothy 2:4 (ESV), "**...our savior, who desires all men to be saved and to come to the knowledge of the truth.**" I urge you do not count anybody out by thinking they are too far away from God. Nobody is too far lost to be redeemed by Jesus Christ. "**...he is patient with you, not wanting anyone to perish, but everyone to come to repentance.**" (2 Peter 3:9). That is a beautiful truth that we should cherish and hold onto during the difficult times when we struggle to help those of the world.

Being a member of God's team means we must be patient with other people who deny God's existence. Our goal should be to live a life that proves God's existence every single day through our words and our actions. We do that by not only loving our teammates who are believers, but also loving our enemies who are not believers. Jesus said, **"But I tell you, love your enemies and pray for those who persecute you..."** (Matthew 5:44). God wants us to be different and to intentionally love those who are against us. God is patient with them, and so we should be too.

"Don't use foul or abusive language. Let everything you say be good and helpful, so that your words will be an encouragement to those who hear them." (Ephesians 4:29 NLT). Soften their hearts with kind words, before you plant the mustard seed of God's Kingdom. Your teammates need to see Christ's love in you before they will be able to recognize the love that is found in Jesus. Remember, that you play a very significant role on God's team, and you should take responsibility of your words and actions to help grow God's kingdom.

WASH ONE ANOTHER'S UNIFORMS

In John chapter 13, just before Jesus was betrayed by one of His own teammates, He took water in a basin and began to wash the feet of His disciples. Then He said to one of them who did not understand what He was doing, **"Unless I wash you, you have no part with me."** (John 13:8). Jesus knew that He had to be the ONE to wash us clean in order for us to understand His abounding grace, mercy and love.

In verse 12, after Jesus washed and dried His disciples' feet He said to them, **"Do you understand what I have**

done for you? Now that I, your Lord and Teacher, have washed your feet, you also should wash one another's feet." (John 13:12,14). In other words, now that God has washed us free from sin and made us clean through forgiveness, we should also forgive each other and love one another in the same way.

We must practice forgiveness and compassion because that is the Christ-like way of living this life. In life, people will make mistakes against us, betray us, or make us upset because of something they did or said. As Christians, we look past their faults and see the beauty in them. We put these scriptural principles into action on the baseball field, in the classroom, at home, at our jobs, and everywhere else. Even though people are flawed humans and make mistakes, we show them compassion by forgiving them and making all things new. That is what Christ did and it is a beautiful way to live.

BE A LIGHT

When you are playing baseball, one thing is for certain; you need light to be able to see the baseball. When the sun goes down, unless the field has lights, you will no longer be able to play. Yet, if the field does have lights and they are turned on, you will see clearly again, and you be able to continue playing. As a Christian, you are a spiritual light whose job it is to shine bright so that others can see Christ through you. Baseball gives us a tremendous platform to be seen and heard by others. Let us embrace that truth and shine bright for others to see Christ. Jesus put it this way, **"No one lights a lamp and then hides it or puts it under a basket. Instead, a lamp is placed on a stand, where its light can be seen by all who enter the house."** (Luke 11:33).

Remember, you never know who is watching you and your actions will always speak louder than your words. Baseball is a great game to discipline our actions because we are constantly being challenged with tough situations. It may be a terrible call from an umpire, or something a player does or says to you. As a baseball player, you must become aware of the fact that other people are watching you while you are on the baseball field. Every gesture you make or word you speak is potentially seen or heard by somebody else—from the way you carry yourself out on the field, to the way you react to a bad call from the umpire.

I urge you, baseball brethren, to control your emotions and temper because your actions on a baseball field will be the tell-tale sign of the type of character you have on the inside of you. Be sure to remember your new identity in Christ in whom you represent and play for. **"Therefore, since we are surrounded by such a great cloud of witnesses, let us throw off everything that hinders and the sin that so easily entangles. And let us run with perseverance the race marked out for us, fixing our eyes on Jesus, the pioneer and perfecter of faith."** (Hebrews 12:1-2).

Whether you realize this to be true or not, baseball players are natural born leaders. Whether some use that role for good or evil is up to the individual player. As a Christian baseball player, baseball is the perfect opportunity to show other people the love of Christ, which you have received and enjoy through your faith. Show them that light is better than darkness, that faith is better than doubt, that a savior is better than hopelessness. If you are not leading the way by following Jesus, then you will become a follower of somebody who is leading you into darkness.

Therefore, let us hold on to Christ's love and grace and lead the way to righteousness by following Christ. Let us not allow any petty or insignificant situation in a baseball game misrepresent who we are in Christ. **"...so that you may prove what the will of God is, that which is good and acceptable and perfect."** (Romans 12:2 NASB).

For FREE interactive videos inside of a private membership site visit: http://baseballgenesisbook.com/member

Team Culture

CHAPTER

4

DEVELOPING A STRATEGY

As a player in this game of life, it is very important to know who we play for. That way we can stand up for what we believe in and be firm in the values that the team represents. Just as important, is to know who we are playing against. In the same way, we can know what we stand against and what we need to avoid. In baseball, we use strategy to outwit and outperform our opponent every pitch and play. We do this because we know that our opponent is also trying their best to defeat us. Let us then be strategic in knowing who we are, and the tactics that we are up against in this spiritual battle of Good vs. Evil.

SCOUTING REPORT

To understand that there are two teams competing for spiritual victory in our lives is the first step towards a victorious spiritual life. God is the head coach of Team Righteousness, and Satan is the head coach of Team

Lawlessness. The world we live in is the home field of Satan's Team of Lawlessness and it will continue to be that way until the return of our Lord and Savior Jesus Christ. **"But, according to his promise, we are waiting for new heavens and a new earth, in which righteousness truly resides."** (2 Peter 3:13 ESV).

These two teams have very different mindsets and approaches to life. It is important that we understand the strategies our opponent is using to attack us so that we can defend against it. **"Be alert and of sober mind. Your enemy the devil prowls around like a roaring lion looking for someone to devour."** (1 Peter 5:8). Satan's team will try their best to get us out and attack us wherever we show weakness. This is why if we can understand our opponent's approach and strategy in advance, like a scouting report, it will give us a huge advantage towards victory.

In high school and college, Satan had a very detailed scouting report on me and he knew where I was weak and vulnerable to be attacked and defeated. Like a pitcher who knew how to get me out, Satan would tempt me with the same lust-filled temptations every day. I had to recognize that these pleasure seeking temptations were attempts to seek and destroy me and my future in Christ. I knew I was sinning and striking out because I would feel a very heavy weight and burden on my chest after committing a sinful act. I had to recognize for myself that those pitches were not within the strike zone and I had to learn to lay off of them.

Satan and his team will throw us pitches that look enticing to swing at, like a curve ball that will dip out of the zone at the last second. Let us get great at recognizing those pitches and even slow down the game when necessary. Imagine if you had the ability to slow down the game and freeze a baseball that was being thrown your way. Do you think you would have a much better chance at swinging at pitches within the strike zone and laying off of those bad pitches? In life, we can choose to slow down our decisions and analyze the consequences of our choices.

As soon as you get out of bed in the morning, you are digging in the batter's box of life. So be ready for pitches that will come your way that day. Soon the Devil will have a detailed scouting report on you as well, and will know how to pitch you for the best chances of getting you out. So be cautious and disciplined to recognize what pitches you struggle with the most and make the necessary adjustments to improve in those areas. Sometimes it will be the pitch of lust, or of greed, or of disobeying our parents. It is important to know yourself, as a player, so that you can work to lay off of those tough pitches and look for something that is within the strike zone. Remember, we cannot determine what pitches are thrown our way, but we can choose which pitches we will swing at and take action on.

Like in baseball, a good tip is to keep your head clear of the noise and negativity that can come from the opponent's dugout, or from the crowd. Be confident in the Lord as your head coach, and keep His promises and blessings in the forefront of your mind. Write them down on the bill of your hat and remember verses that will strengthen you throughout your day. Watch out for those curve balls of perverted images, lies, and earthly temptations that will cross your mind daily. All you have to do is let them go by, like a bad pitch, and look for the next pitch. Only take action on those pitches that are within the strike zone, and remember all that your coach has taught you.

MAKING ADJUSTMENTS

In baseball and in life, you will have some good days and you will have some bad days. You will have days which you will feel on top of the world. Other days you will feel defeated by the opponent. Some days you will be able to recognize every pitch from out of the pitcher's hand. Other days, you will be filled with doubt and fear at the plate of life. Some days you will feel like MVP, and other days you will find yourselves in a sin slump and will feel undeserving to be on God's team. When we do find ourselves in a sin slump, it is important to slow down, focus on Jesus, and make the proper adjustments.

In baseball, we are told from a very young age to keep our eyes on the baseball or else we will strike out or make an error. In Christianity, we are told to keep our eyes on Jesus or we will inevitably fall back into sin. If we wish to be a great player for Christ, it is important to remember to fix our eyes on Jesus and always keep Him in our thoughts. Recalling who He is and the love He provides for us daily. Whenever we are tempted to sin, or get angry and want to act out, we must remember to keep our eyes focused on the baseball of life who is Jesus Christ. **"We do this by keeping our eyes on Jesus, the champion who initiates and perfects our faith."** (Hebrews 12:2 NLT).

Adjustments are a big part of the game of baseball and a big part of the Christian life. If we do not make the proper adjustments in this game of life, we will find ourselves striking out and making errors over and over again. This will be detrimental for us, our family, and our team. For example, in baseball if you keep striking out because you continue to let your weight get out in front of you on a change-up, you have to take note of it and make a proper adjustment to keep your weight back. If you do not make the adjustment, you will continue to strike out, and you will be hurting yourself and your team.

Personally, I had to make some major adjustments in my life once I became a follower of Jesus Christ. I was living a life of sin and was making bad choices that I did not want to make, but I would continue to make them. Like Paul who said, **"For I do not understand my own actions. For I do not do what I want, but I do the very thing I hate."** (Romans 7:15 ESV). I had to seek the strength from God to open his Word for encouragement and instruction. Slowly I was being coached, and finally I started to see results. It continues to take discipline day in and day out to be the best player of life that I can be for Christ. Yet, the important thing is that I am improving and I know who I play for and which team I represent. It is my hope to be the best player I can in life for my coach Jesus Christ and my team of believers in God.

CONFESS TO EACH OTHER

Baseball and life are games of discipline, sacrifice, and adjustments. Yes, there will be days when we get fooled and swing outside of the strike zone, it happens in baseball and it will happen in life. What we cannot do is continue to make the same mistake over and over again. At that point when we do find ourselves in a slump of sin, it is crucial to find a teammate that we can confess our sin to. We do this so that we can be held accountable, and your teammate will be able to work with you to make the proper adjustment. **"Therefore confess your sins to each other and pray for each other so that you may be healed."** (James 5:16).

In baseball, when we need help to improve in an area in the game, we ask a teammate to work with us to make us better. It works the same way in life, and it is important to find a Christian teammate who you can trust to help you and keep you accountable. In return, you should help him and keep him accountable. It is like having a throwing partner in life, you confess to each other and you become better because of it. We must continue to improve our skills in this game, improve our relationship with our teammates, our coach, and improve our ability to recognize tough pitches so that we can better support our team and the mission. Such is true in baseball, and such is true in life.

We are not born into this world knowing how to play this game of life properly, that is why we must practice, be coachable, seek guidance, and make the proper adjustments as we continue to move forward. Receiving the instruction from our coach and the accountability from a teammate to make the proper adjustments are very critical elements to our Christian walks. We all want to be significant players for God, therefore we must put in the time and trust in His process. **"...being confident of this, that he who began a good work in you will carry it on to completion until the day of Christ Jesus."** (Philippians 1:6).

PRAYER AND MEDITATION

God is willing to help us become the greatest players that we can be, we just have to spend time with Him in prayer and meditation so that we can be coached by Him. I remember when I first began to meditate by sitting still in silence for a period of 5-20 minutes. It gave me so much peace of mind and serenity, as I felt the presence of God comfort me. As I sat there, I called to remembrance God's promises and His subtle presence would give me great insight on how to live a better life. **"I will meditate on your precepts and fix my eyes on your ways."** (Psalm 119:15). I desire the same experience for you in this life. So make it a priority to spend time with God in prayer and in meditation remembering who God is and who you are in the eyes of God, while you listen and wait for His subtle guidance.

For FREE interactive videos inside of a private membership site visit: http://baseballgenesisbook.com/member

CHAPTER

5

HAVING AN APPROACH

As Christian baseball players we must keep Jesus as the cornerstone of our lives. Similar to home plate being the cornerstone on the baseball field in which everything else on the field is placed around. Jesus is the cornerstone of our lives. **"And the cornerstone is Christ Jesus himself."** (Ephesians 2:20 NLT). This declaration can help us determine the directions we will go in our lives. Every decision we make needs to align with the cornerstone, Jesus Christ, because He in fact is **"...the way, the truth, and the life."** (John 14:16 NLT). Jesus proved that statement to be true through His life, death, and resurrection from the dead. Jesus confirmed that He was the Son of God, and that everything He said was the truth.

Remember that we are new creations and our old ways have passed away. Our prior ways of thinking and acting need to be diminished, and righteousness needs to increase. **"He must increase, but I must decrease."** (John 3:30

ESV). Everything can change from the inside out because the kingdom of God is within you. The Holy Spirit is within you guiding you and convicting you when you do commit an error. So listen to your heart and let Christ's love shine through you! **"For God has not given us a spirit of fear and timidity, but of power, love, and self-discipline."** (2 Timothy 1:7 NLT).

RENEWING OF YOUR MIND

We have to remember that we once played on Team Lawlessness, but now we are on Team Righteousness and have a new way to approach this game of life. God tells us in Romans 12:2 (NASB) **"...do not be conformed to this world, but be transformed by the renewing of your mind."** For we were once members of the opposition: filthy in sin, doubt, and filled with impure thoughts and images. As Christians, we have to put away the old ways of doing things and focus on renewing our minds daily through reading God's Word and praying because prayer has power to reconcile us with our coach, who is God.

Just because we are Christians does not mean we will not still hear the voice of our former ruler, Satan. Satan will try to taunt us in every which way he can to convince us that we are not worthy to be called righteous. Just do not listen to that voice any longer. Like an obnoxious baseball fan in the stands, you ignore it and stay in tune to the voice of your new coach, God, who loves you unconditionally like a loving-father.

STAY IN TUNE WITH GOD

Let us become imitators of God's very own heart. Whatever breaks God's heart, should break our hearts as well. Whatever brings God's heart joy should bring our hearts joy as well. Knowing God not only with our minds, but with our hearts will give us clarity on what is right and what is wrong. Having God's heart will help us become more like His Son Jesus. Let us be like a baseball player who already knows his coach's thoughts before he speaks them.

SING SONGS OF PRAISE

As a Christian, I encourage you to listen to worship music daily because it will give you strength and will renew your mind with positive inspiration and encouragement. In the Bible it talks many times about singing songs of praise from your heart to the Lord. **"Shout to the LORD, all the earth; break out in praise and sing for joy!"** (Psalm 98:4 NLT). From my own experiences, worshiping God through songs of praise and singing them out loud on the baseball field can bring a tremendous amount of gratitude and joy that will fill the field with love. I encourage you to try this out and see the impact that it will have. Others will see your joy pouring out of you and they will want to experience what you have in Christ.

Yes, many of your teammates and peers in the world will be listening to and singing songs of lust, greed, drugs, violence, and other worldly desires, but you my friend know that you must be transformed by the renewal of your mind. You will be more adapt to sing songs that praise His glory and goodness **"...now that you have tasted that the Lord is good."** (1Peter 2:3). Therefore, you will begin to love feeding your mind with Godly music and singing songs of praise that embrace His Word. I sincerely promise that you will feel a huge difference in your life when you do. I truly believe this act alone will impact your life greatly!

PLAYING THROUGH THE EYES OF GOD

We are truly blessed to play this game of baseball. Let us not take this opportunity for granted one single day. Let us play the game with full effort and play it properly, not because your baseball coach or your parents are watching you, but because your creator in heaven is watching you.

If you could see the game through God's eyes, would he be pleased with you? The actions you take, the words you say, would God be happy with your progress? Let us start to recognize who we truly play for and start playing for Him today!

HOW TO SCORE

In baseball and in life, our mission is to score runs. It is obvious how we score runs in baseball—we get on, we get over, and we get in. In life, our objective is to do the same. We will get on, get over, and get in, then help others to do the same. Now let us understand what it means to accomplish those three steps in our lives.

In order to get on first base, we have to first step into the batter's box of faith. That means we have to believe that **"For God so loved the world that he gave his one and only Son, that whoever believes in him shall not perish but have eternal life."** (John 3:16). Once you believe in your heart this foundational truth, then you have officially made solid contact with God. Once you put that foundational truth into play, you can then run down the line and reach first base, which is simply called, 'Justification'.

In simple terms, justification means that justice has been served and punishment has been paid for our sins once and for all, past, present, and future. **"God made him who had no sin to be sin for us, so that in him we might become the righteousness of God."** (2 Corinthians 5:21). There is a great transfer of identity that happens at this point. Our sinful identity is traded for the righteousness of Jesus. This is only possible because the price of our sin has been paid for by Jesus who knew no sin, yet became sin for us, and suffered the severe punishment of sin on the cross. **"...and all are justified freely by his grace through the redemption that came by Christ Jesus."** (Romans 3:24). We were not worthy of this free gift, but because of Jesus we have been made worthy!

Once we have a firm foundation in our 'Justification' and live it out as a saved people who are made righteous and worthy before God, then we can get our lead and move towards second base. Second base is called, 'Sanctification' which simply means to become more and more like Jesus. Jesus was a holy and perfect role model for us to follow. To become more like Jesus means we are becoming more pure, holy, and righteous. In order to do this effectively we need to grow in a relationship with Jesus by reading His word, praying daily, and practicing what He preaches.

Once we go through sanctification, **"He must increase, but I must decrease."** (John 3:30 ESV), then we can head toward third base which is known as 'Glorification'. This is the final step of the transformation process where God's work is finished and has removed sin from us making us perfect, mature, and complete.

Once we reach glorification, Jesus meets us at the third base coaching box and waves us home. We head home to heaven, another run is added to the board, and we get to celebrate with our teammates who have reached home before us. **"Similarly, anyone who competes as an athlete does not receive the victor's crown except by competing according to the rules."** (2 Timothy 2:5). The way to get to heaven is through faith alone in Christ alone–through justification, sanctification, and glorification.

GETTING PICKED OFF

Be aware that your opponent is trying to stop you from reaching home and will make attempts to pick you off base. Getting picked off base in baseball is extremely detrimental to you and to your team. In life, it is the same. You must be sure not to get picked off while on base in life by staying close to the Word of God. The Bible represents the bases and when we remain close to or in contact with the Bible, we are safe. When we drift too far away from the Bible, it becomes easy for us to get picked off. Let us remember to stay close to God's Word and stay in contact with Him so that we can stay on course and receive the victor's crown.

HOW WE WIN

We win by scoring runs and by helping our teammates get on, get over, and get in with us. Jesus introduced this idea to His disciples before He ascended into heaven. He said, **"Go, therefore and make disciples of all nations...teaching them to observe everything I have commanded you."** (Matthew 28:18,20 ESV). What Jesus was actually telling His team was to go out there and get some R.B.I.'s! Get people on base, get them over, and get them in safely.

We should take tremendous joy in introducing people to Jesus, so that they can be on a victorious team on this journey of life. People need the confidence to walk themselves up to the batter's box of faith to seek the knowledge of God. We can help by giving them the confidence to do so. Once they do have that courage, it is then our duty to cheer them on and do our best to get them on, get them over, and get them in. It is a simple process, yet it is not always an easy one. It says in James chapter 5, **"Whoever turns a sinner from the error of their way will**

save them from death and cover over a multitude of sins." (V. 20).

It will certainly be worth our while to do as Jesus instructs for us to do because it will create the utmost satisfaction and joy in our Christian walks. To know and accept Jesus Christ as Lord and Savior is the single biggest decision each and every one of us will have to make in this lifetime. Once we make that decision, whether we play for Him or against Him, will determine our eternal resting place.

For FREE interactive videos inside of a private membership site visit: http://baseballgenesisbook.com/member

CHAPTER

6

TRAINING FOR GODLINESS

If we desire to succeed within the game of baseball and glorify God with our play, we are going to have to push ourselves physically, mentally, and spiritually passed our own limitations. If we can push ourselves passed our own limitations and endure the pain that will be involved, we will reach new heights and inevitably grow stronger in all areas. **"I consider that our present sufferings are not worth comparing with the glory that will be revealed in us."** (Romans 8:18).

When training for baseball, it would be advantageous to you to remind yourself of Jesus and the pain and sacrifice that He endured for us that day on Calvary Hill. All of the blood, the sweat, the tears that He shed for us so that we could receive the free gift of eternal life. So while you are in the midst of painstaking training for baseball, do your best to tap into that memory of His sacrifice so that you can gain a tremendous strength boost. **"I can do all things through Him who strengthens me."** (Philippians 4:13 NASB).

As a follower of Jesus, you have the memory of Calvary Hill to recall whenever you feel like giving up. With sweat coming down your face and blood dripping from open wounds, use the power of Jesus Christ to push you passed your own limiting beliefs, pain, and struggle. **"...he endured the cross, scorning its shame, and sat down at the right hand of the throne of God. Consider him who endured such opposition from sinners, so that you will not grow weary and lose heart."** (Hebrews 12:2).

DEVELOP YOUR TALENTS INTO GIFTS

God has given each and every one of us who play this game of baseball a tremendous amount of talent. Through this game God has given us joy, friends, and experiences that shape our reality and character. It is time for us to give back to God. **"Each of you should use whatever gift you have received to serve others, as faithful stewards of God's grace in its various forms."** (1 Peter 4:10).

If you wish to glorify God with your play you are going to need to develop your talents through training, practicing daily, and becoming a great teammate. It is up to us to develop our talents into something greater as OUR gift TO God. Let us use God's love as the fuel that burns inside of us and empowers us to reach new heights in becoming even greater Christian baseball players than we could have ever imagined. We can do this because our love for God first came because He first loved us. **"Love the LORD your God with all your heart and with all your soul and with all your strength."** (Deuteronomy 6:5).

TRAINING FOR GODLINESS

Godliness is truly what we are after as Christians in this lifetime, and it is absolutely something that we need to train for. **"Physical training is good, but training for godliness is much better, promising benefits in this life and in the life to come."** (1 Timothy 4:8 NLT). Godliness does not just happen by accident, for godliness comes from a training regimen that many of us neglect to perform, but I would like to encourage you to begin training for godliness today.

Baseball and Christianity are very similar in the fact that you must practice and train on a consistent basis if you wish to see any improvements in the skills necessary to be successful. Training for godliness is like a baseball workout program, it is necessary to warm up properly through prayer and petition, stretch our faith through relying on God's promises, and develop strong spiritual muscle through acting on faith and applying what is written in Scripture.

SPIRITUAL TRAINING

We train our muscles to get stronger physically, and mentally we train our minds to gather more knowledge, but most people neglect the spiritual training needed to gain wisdom through a personal relationship with God. Like our physical bodies and our minds, our spiritual bodies also need the proper amount of food, water, exercise and rejuvenation as well.

"Then Jesus declared, 'I am the bread of life. Whoever comes to me will never go hungry, and whoever believes in me will never be thirsty.'" (John 6:35). Jesus said that He is the bread of life and that we should not survive on bread alone, but on every word that comes from God. He also says that He is the living water. **"...whoever drinks the water I give them will never thirst. Indeed, the water I give them will become in them a spring of water welling up to eternal life."** (John 4:14). This water which Jesus is speaking of is spiritual water for our spiritual bodies. This water is accessible by staying close to Jesus and absorbing His grace, love, and mercy.

We could easily lose the fight of faith by refusing to train or neglecting to nourish our bodies with this spiritual food and water. **"Blessed are those who hunger and thirst for righteousness, for they will be filled."** (Matthew 5:6). Let us not be like those who neglect to nourish their spiritual bodies. Let us hunger and thirst for the purity and excellences of life found in Jesus!

Training spiritually involves consistent practice and dedication through tough and difficult seasons. Like any other training program, it takes time to develop the strength in order to see any noticeable results. This is not a quick fix process, but it is a worthwhile process for you to put forth your full trust, dedication, and effort.

MY TESTIMONY

For me, my life changed abruptly on a sunny Thursday afternoon, when I found myself lying on the ground of the warning track of a college baseball field. I was screaming in pain, and squeezing the hand of the closest teammate for comfort, as the rest of my team ran over to surround me. Players and students began to pray over me, hoping that I would be okay. It was at that moment when I felt an unforgettable feeling that I had never experienced before. It was a feeling of reassurance, and I knew it was God telling me that everything would be okay. It was at that moment when I put my full trust in God.

Just seconds prior, I was playing center field during a scrimmage game when a fly ball was hit to deep right-center field. I got a great jump on the ball and I tracked it down just one step away from the brick wall that was in center field. I ran full speed right into that brick wall with no padding, full blast with my knee and the left side of my face. I was in severe pain, but did not know the severity of it until the doctor had seen me hours later.

I was immediately rushed to the hospital to soon find out that I had a completely broken patella bone, or knee cap, and a fractured sinus cavity in my face. I would have emergency surgery that night to put my kneecap back together, and I was told I would be out of the game of baseball for a significant amount of time.

It was always my dream as a kid to play in the Major Leagues. I did not fully realize it then, but baseball was an idol to me because it was all that I would think about. I worshiped the game of baseball as if it was the only thing that mattered in my life. I had my identity wrapped up in baseball because most of my joy came from baseball, and all my effort was put into baseball.

Although I had big dreams to play baseball professionally, God had better plans for my life. God took baseball away from me many times throughout my career through injuries, so that I could get closer to him and drink the spiritual water and eat the spiritual bread that I needed so desperately. God was breaking me down so that I could grow stronger in faith and depend more on Jesus for true fulfillment and satisfaction.

During that time of recovery, I poured into God's Word at Arizona Christian University. I became grateful in the face of sorrow. A new spiritual well was overflowing from my soul. I would go to chapels twice a week and sing worship songs of praise, thanking God for restoring my faith in His Son Jesus. For I knew God had plans to restore me back to perfect health and to make it possible for me to impact my team for Jesus. I knew that God never made mistakes, and that this tribulation was going to be used for His glory to grow God's kingdom through the game.

I rejoined the team just four months after the accident to the surprise of many people who had witnessed. I had an incredible remainder of the baseball season in 2013, and even though the team was filled with sin, I had developed a few strong relationships with my fellow teammates. We made it all the way to a Christian College World Series and the season ended in dramatic fashion when I hit a walk-off home run in an elimination game in that tournament. It kept our hopes alive for one more day, as the season ended on my birthday, May 17th. I am eternally grateful for the gift that God had given me through this transformational season of my life.

I do not tell you this story to boast about myself and my abilities, but I tell it to boast about God and His ability to use a sinner like me, to glorify Him through the game of baseball. God had used this challenge in my life to give me a new perspective and a reality check that God is the one who is in control. I could not possibly do anything or go anywhere by myself. I was reminded to include God and allow His will to be done in my life. A precious and meaningful truth that I hope you will take with you.

God gave me a new sense of gratitude for the gift of life, a healthy body, and the talents of playing the game of baseball. He took something broken and ugly and made it new and useful. My life has never been the same since that season of my life. I went from trying to glorify myself through the game of baseball and striving to make it to the big leagues, to acknowledging that God is one who is ultimately in control, and I am here to help spread the good news of the Gospel of Jesus Christ in order to make Him famous. I am eternally grateful for the trials that God has orchestrated in my life so that I could learn, grow, and accomplish what He has in store for me to accomplish in this life. Glory be to God!

RESPONDING BY FAITH

Whether you choose to believe it or not, there will be trials, tribulations, and setbacks in your own life that will impact your faith. How you respond to those circumstances in life is what will ultimately make you bitter or will make you better. It is important to remember to keep your focus on Jesus and the heavenly future that He promises is in store for you.

Whenever you are in a difficult season of your life it is so important to think about "...**whatever is true, whatever is noble, whatever is right, whatever is pure, whatever is lovely, whatever is admirable–if anything is excellent or praiseworthy–think about such things.**" (Philippians 4:8). God is an excellent coach who wants what is best for you in the long-run. Never forget that role of God in your life. Life may seem tough at times, but through testing of your faith is the only way to develop your faith.

Always remember God's faithful promises when you are in a tough season of your life, on or off the baseball field.

Remember to always lean on Him and trust in Him that He has great and wonderful plans for your future. Always respond to all circumstances with faith and a positive attitude. Only then will you succeed in your faith walk and become an impact player on God's team.

FAITH IS A MUSCLE

Did you know that faith is like a muscle in your body? You have to use it in order to develop it, make it stronger, and overall more effective. Like the old saying goes, "If you don't use it, you lose it". The same goes for your faith and its effectiveness! So it is important to practice and apply your faith whenever you get the opportunity to do so. You can apply faith while you are weight training, at baseball practice, and during your baseball season.

When I had my knee surgery back in September of 2012, the surgeon reconstructed my knee cap using two screws and a metal wire. My leg was put in a straight-legged splint for six weeks where I was not able to move my leg or put any of my bodyweight on it. I used crutches to get around, and I was not able to use my leg at all for those six weeks.

What happened after six weeks of not using my leg was something called atrophy. Atrophy is when you do not use a muscle for a long period of time and its strength and ability to work effectively diminish. When I was finally able to remove the splint, I discovered that I had lost most of my leg muscles. I had to build back enough strength to sustain my body weight, and I had to relearn how to walk again. It was a long and strenuous process in physical therapy that took a lot of patience and consistent effort to see any results.

Eventually, the strength and the muscle did grow back, and I was able to walk, run, jump, and play baseball again. I was so grateful to learn the effectiveness of patience and consistency while keeping focus on the end goal. Just like when Paul said, **"I press on toward the goal for the prize of the upward call of God in Christ Jesus."** (Philippians 3:14 ESV). Paul was very determined to complete his ministry as he pressed forward through the struggle everyday by keeping his eye on the most glorious of prizes, his reward for fulfilling to grow Christ's Church.

DEALING WITH FAILURE

I believe there is no better opportunity to grow in your faith than within the game of baseball. It is a game of failure, where if you fail seven out of ten times then you are considered great. Keeping this in mind, I urge you to use every trial that you face as an opportunity to put your faith to the test so that it can grow stronger. Whether that trial be a slump, an error, a strikeout, or an injury, remember to always use your trial to your advancement and to take your faith to the next level.

"Consider it all joy, my brethren, when you encounter various trials, knowing that the TESTING OF YOUR FAITH produces endurance. And let endurance have its perfect result, so that you may be perfect and complete, lacking in nothing...." (James 1:3-5 NASB)

God wants us to use these trials that we face as a way to exercise and increase our faith. I encourage you to believe in the promise that you are going through hard times in order to develop your faith and make it stronger for your good. Use faith daily to propel you through those difficult times, reminding yourself that "...for those who love God all things work together for good, for those who are called according to his purpose." (Romans 8:28 ESV). This is a significant truth that we must hold onto if we wish to grow substantially in our faith.

God will never do anything to harm you without a purpose or cause behind it. Remember, God wants you to be a success, not a failure. How God makes this happen is through the testing of your faith, through trials and tribulations that we go through in our lives. How you respond to them is your choice and will determine the growth of your faith.

FAITH IS THE KEY

Having a strong faith and a healthy spiritual body has the ability not only to improve your life greatly, but your baseball career as well. It is the missing ingredient for many baseball players who desire to increase their baseball performance. The substance of faith truly has power to do remarkable things in the physical and spiritual realms, on and off the baseball field.

Many players have not developed their faith strong enough to use it properly when they need it the most. When things get tough on the baseball field, faith has the ability to pull you out of those situations and see a brighter future. If you have faith and you sense anger or frustration coming to the surface, you will know how to control your emotions and direct it in a positive direction.

Using failure or setbacks as fuel to propel you forward is the very key to becoming a very successful person on and off the baseball field. When you discover this key to unlocking your full potential through strong faith in a loving God, you will become a much stronger person and a much greater baseball player as a result. Believe and you will achieve in Jesus Christ. Let us begin using faith to be great at baseball, and use baseball to be great at faith.

For FREE interactive videos inside of a private membership site visit: http://baseballgenesisbook.com/member

CHAPTER

7

LIVING AS WORLD CHAMPIONS

In baseball, there are nine innings in a game. If you are fortunate to stay in the game long enough, you will play all nine innings. Sometimes, players get taken out early due to committing costly errors, or simply an unfortunate situation that occurs. There are also times when players will go into extra innings, and the game will continue for a little bit longer than expected.

In life, there are also nine innings of play. Each inning represents a decade, or ten years of a human being's life. Most healthy human beings can live to the age of ninety years old, which we would call a full life. You never know how long you will play in this game of life, but that is not what is important. What is important is how hard you play while you are in the game, and for whom you play for.

This spiritual battle that we all face is not over until the return of Jesus Christ to this earth, or until we meet Him on our Judgment Day. So whether you are nine years old, or ninety years old, you must remember to continue to battle and: **"Fight the good fight of the faith. Take hold of the eternal life to which you were called when you made your good confession in the presence of many witnesses."** (1 Timothy 6:12). I urge you, baseball brethren, to continue to fight the good fight, day in and day out for the Christian team by playing your specific position to the best of your God-given ability.

PLAYING YOUR POSITION

Remember that God is the ultimate head coach and authority in our lives. He decides who plays what position, when, and for how long. We are simply the players and our duty is to play our positions to the best of our abilities when we are given the opportunity to do so. Remember, God does not expect us to be perfect, but He does expect us to give Him our best effort. **"Do your best to present yourself to God as one approved, a worker who does not need to be ashamed and who correctly handles the word of truth."** (2 Timothy 2:15).

Our mission is to help our team win by scoring runs and being a significant player on the team. As the church, we need to pick each other up, and play our positions well so that our team will succeed. Again, we do not have the power to choose where we are born, at which particular time in history, and to what family and body we are born into. All of those positions were predestined and chosen for us before time. **"But even before I was born, God chose me**

and called me by his marvelous grace." (Galatians 1:15 NLT). All we have the ability to do is develop ourselves and play our positions to the best of our abilities. Our positions will sometimes change from time to time with the schools we attend, the baseball teams we play for, and the neighborhoods we live in, but the goal still remains the same—win players to Christ.

When we are living in this world, it is so critical to remember to keep your focus on what this book is all about—keeping your focus on Jesus. If you keep your focus on Jesus you will make the right play when temptations come your way. As a result of making the right play, you will live a more successful and victorious life as you walk with Christ on this journey.

CROWNED WORLD CHAMPIONS

As Christians, it is important to remember daily who you are declared to be by God—a conqueror of the world. Jesus has already crowned us World Champions of life because of what He did for us. He lived a perfect life, yet suffered and died in our place for the consequences of sin. Three days later He rose from the grave and defeated sin and death once and for all. **"...in all these things WE are more than conquerors through HIM who loved us."** (Romans 8:37). We are champions because of what Jesus has done for us, and for accepting His free gift to join His team by faith, and not by our works.

Jesus won the game for us and now that we are on His team and we wear the Jerseys of Righteousness, we too get to celebrate as World Champions in life. As World Champions, our desire should be to play like a champion, and not play like our former ways of sin and disobedience. **"For you have spent enough time in the past doing what pagans choose to do—living in debauchery, lust, drunkenness, orgies, carousing and detestable idolatry."** (1 Peter 4:3). Our desire should be to play like the champions that we already are in Christ through His redemption. Seeing ourselves the way God sees us will begin to transform us from the inside out into Christ-likeness.

Jesus has certainly given us the golden principles needed to live a victorious life in this world. As long as we come to know Jesus and follow Him for who He truly is, we will reign victoriously. His teachings are true, powerful, and will benefit you in every aspect of your life.

I hope the message in this book has served you to embrace the faith and to use the strength found in Jesus Christ. May God's love abide in you as you embrace yourself rightfully as a champion through Jesus Christ. May the peace and mercy of our Lord Jesus Christ give you the strength of a new identity and a purpose for life that you have found in Him!

For FREE interactive videos inside of a private membership site visit: http://baseballgenesisbook.com/member

A Prayer To Accept Jesus Christ
AS YOUR LORD AND SAVIOR

If you have not yet accepted Jesus Christ as your Lord and Savior through faith, then here is a short prayer for you to say out loud or to yourself that will declare your repentance and acceptance onto God's team.

Dear God,

I fully acknowledge that I have been a sinner all of my life. I have disobeyed you and turned my back against you many times. Today, I fully repent of my sins and of my ways. I fully acknowledge your Son Jesus Christ, whom came down to earth to save sinners like myself from destruction. I fully accept the gift of grace and mercy that your Son Jesus has purchased for me and for others. I believe in the power of His name and I accept Jesus Christ into my life as my Lord and Savior. I believe that Jesus died for my sins once and for all. I am so thankful for this free gift of grace and mercy. Lord I am fully yours to use me as you please. Train me up to be a significant player as a Christ follower. In Jesus name I pray. Amen!

Congratulations teammate! You are now a World Champion in life! Go now and share the good news with others!

For further information

To get the latest training resources from Trevor Santor and Baseball Genesis visit the website at **www.baseballgenesis.com**, also 'Like' and 'Follow' @baseballgenesis on your favorite social networks: Facebook, Twitter, YouTube, Instagram, and Tumblr.

ABOUT THE AUTHOR

Trevor Santor is a devoted Christian faith baseball coach who played collegiate baseball at Grand Canyon University (2009-2012) and Arizona Christian University (2012-2014). Trevor adopted the grand vision of *Growing God's Kingdom Through the Game of Baseball* after a severe accident when he ran into a brick wall in the outfield to make a catch in September of 2012. He hopes to empower other baseball players to follow Jesus by teaching the Christian faith through the game of baseball. Trevor founded Baseball Genesis in 2013. He currently coaches high school baseball in Phoenix, Arizona and does ministry work at his local church, Jr. High, and high schools around the valley.